The ALL TIME BEST Collection

VOLUME ONE

Compiled by Mark Mumford
First Published 1994
© International Music Publications Limited
Southend Road, Woodford Green, Essex IG8 8HN, England

215-2-976

BAKER STREET

Words and Music by
GERRY RAFFERTY

Verse 1. Wind-ing your way down on Bak — er Street.

2. This cit-y des — ert makes you feel so cold.__ He's got

4

Verse 3:   Way down the street there's a lot in his place,
            He opens his door he's got that look on his face
            And he asks you where you've been
            You tell him who you've seen and you talk about anything.

Verse 4:   He's got this dream about buyin' some land he's gonna
            Give up the booze and the one night stands and
            Then you'll settle down with some quiet little town
            And forget about everything.

Chorus 3:   But you know you'll always keep movin'
            You know he's never gonna stop movin'
            'Cause he's rollin' he's the rollin' stone.

Chorus 4:   When you wake up it's a new mornin'
            The sun is shinin', it's a new mornin'
            And you're goin', you're goin' home.

BOHEMIAN RHAPSODY

Words and Music by
FREDDIE MERCURY

Did-n't mean to make you cry, If I'm not back a-gain this time to-
I don't want to die, I some-times wish I'd nev-er been born at

mor-row, car-ry on, car-ry on as if noth-ing real-ly mat-ters.

Instrumental Solo

all.

Instrumental Solo

8

10

12

Lyrics: eye._ So you think you can love me and leave me to die._ Oh,_ ba-by,_ can't do this to me, ba-by,_ Just got-ta get out, just got-ta get right out-a here._

Instrumental Solo

poco a poco ritard. e dim.

THE BOYS OF SUMMER

Words and Music by
DON HENLEY and MIKE CAMPBELL

2. I never will forget those nights. I wonder if it was a dream.
    Remember how you made me crazy? Remember how I made you scream?
    Now I don't understand what happened to our love.
    But babe, I'm gonna get you back. I'm gonna show you what I'm made of.

    I can see you, your brown skin shinin' in the sun.
    I see you walkin' real slow and you're smilin' at everyone.
    I can tell you my love for you will still be strong
    After the boys of summer have gone.

3. Out on the road today I saw a "Deadhead" sticker on a Cadillac.
    A little voice inside my head said, "Don't look back. You can never look back."
    I thought I knew what love was. What did I know?
    Those days are gone forever. I should just let 'em go, but

    I can see you, your brown skin shinin' in the sun.
    You got that top pulled down and that radio on, baby.
    And I can tell you my love for you will still be strong
    After the boys of summer have gone.

    I can see you, your brown skin shinin' in the sun.
    You got that hair slicked back and those Wayfarers on, baby.
    I can tell you my love for you will still be strong
    After the boys of summer have gone.

CARELESS WHISPER

Words and Music by
GEORGE MICHAEL
and ANDREW RIDGELEY

CRAZY FOR YOU

Words and Music by
JON LIND and JOHN BETTIS

24

DON'T LET THE SUN GO DOWN ON ME

Words and Music by
ELTON JOHN and BERNIE TAUPIN

DON'T YOU FORGET ABOUT ME

Words and Music by
KEITH FORSEY/STEVE SCHIFF

34

(Will you call my name?) (Come on call my __ name)

Oh will you walk a - way? __ La la la la la __ la la la la __ la la la la la la la la la la.

Repeat ad lib. to Fade

VERSE 2:
Don't you try and pretend
It's my beginning, we'll win in the end.
Oh, harm you or touch your defences,
Vanity, insecurity.
Oh, don't you forget about me,
I'll be alone dancing, you know it baby.
Going to take you apart,
I'll put us back together at heart baby.

END OF THE ROAD

Words and Music by
BABYFACE, L.A. REID
and DARYL SIMMONS

38

Verse 2:
Girl, I know you really love me, you just don't realize.
You've never been there before, it's only your first time.
Maybe I'll forgive you, mmm. . . maybe you'll try.
We should be happy together, forever, you and I.

Bridge 2:
Could you love me again like you loved me before?
This time, I want you to love me much more.
This time, instead just come back to my bed.
And baby, just don't let me down.

Verse 3, spoken:
Girl I'm here for you.
All those times at night when you just hurt me,
And just ran out with that other fellow,
Baby, I knew about it.
I just didn't care.
You just don't understand how much I love you, do you?
I'm here for you.
I'm not out to go out there and cheat all night just like you did, baby.
But that's alright, huh, I love you anyway.
And I'm still gonna be here for you 'til my dyin' day, baby.
Right now, I'm just in so much pain, baby,
'Cause you just won't come back to me, will you?
Just come back to me.

Bridge 3, spoken:
Yes, baby, my heart is lonely.
My heart hurts, baby, yes, I feel pain too.
Baby please . . .

HOLDING BACK THE YEARS

Words by MICK HUCKNALL
Music by MICK HUCKNALL and NEIL MOSS

Hold-ing back the years
Hold-ing back the years
thinking of the
chance for me to es-

fear I've had so long,
-cape from all I know,
when some-bo-dy hears
hold-ing back the tears

42

HEAL THE WORLD

Written and Composed by
MICHAEL JACKSON
Prelude by MARTY PAICH

HOTEL CALIFORNIA

Words and Music by DON FELDER,
DON HENLEY and GLENN FREY

On a dark des-ert high - way, cool wind in my
Her mind is Tif - fa - ny twist - ed. She got the Mer - ce - des

I WILL ALWAYS LOVE YOU

Words and Music by
DOLLY PARTON

You,_____ my dar-ling, you.__ Hmm.__ 2. Bit-ter -

Verses 2, 3, 4:

(Verse 3: Instrumental solo)

sweet mem - o - ries that is__ all_____ I'm tak - ing__ with

me._____ So, good - bye._____ Please, don't__ cry. We both__

To Coda | 1. *To Next Strain* | 2. *D.S. al Coda*

know I'm not what you, you need._____ And I____ 4. I__

...end solo)

60

Verse 3: Instrumental solo

Verse 4:
I hope life treats you kind
And I hope you have all you've dreamed of.
And I wish to you, joy and happiness.
But above all this, I wish you love.
(To Chorus:)

I JUST CALLED TO SAY I LOVE YOU

Words and Music by
STEVIE WONDER

269 - 0 - 23

IMAGINE

Words and Music by
JOHN LENNON

70

RHYTHM IS A DANCER

Words and Music by BENITO BENITES,
JOHN GARRETT III and THEA AUSTIN

RAP:

Let the rhythm ride you, guide you,   sneak inside you, set your mind to move to its pulsation.
When, let it control you   hold you. mould you, not the old,   the new, touch it taste it

Bass vibration, synth sensation   pause, it's not in place   In mind and body must be free to
Free your soul when let it base you   Got to be what you wanna   if the groove don't get you the rhyme flow's

SACRIFICE

Words and Music by
ELTON JOHN and BERNIE TAUPIN

STAIRWAY TO HEAVEN

Words and Music by
JIMMY PAGE and ROBERT PLANT

There's a la-dy who's sure —— all that glit-ters is gold— and she's buy-ing a stair-way— to

Ooh, _____ it makes me won - der.

There's a feel - ing I get _____ when I look to the west, and my spir - it is cry - ing for leav - ing. ____ In my thoughts I have seen rings of smoke through the trees, and the voic - es of those who stand look-

know _____ who shines white light and wants to show _____

how ev-'ry-thing still turns to gold. _____ And if you lis-ten ver-y

hard _____ the tune will come to you _ at last.

When all are one and one is all _____ to be a rock _ and not to

STARS

Words and Music by
MICK HUCKNALL

Moderate Beat, Soulfully

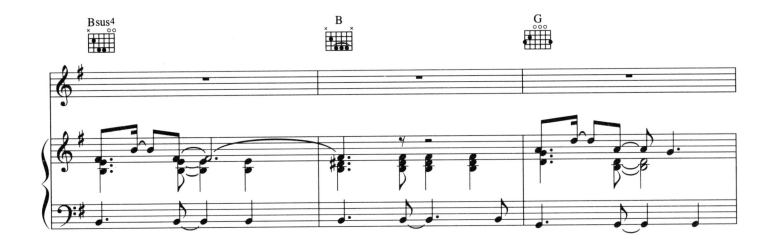

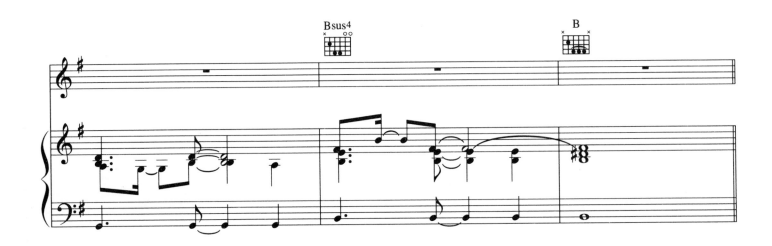

hope you com - pre - hend. _____

Verse 2.

For the man who tried to hurt you,
He's explaining the way I'm feeling.
For all the jealousy I caused you
States the reason why I'm trying to hide.
As for all the things you taught me,
It sends my future into clearer dimensions.
You'll never know how much you hurt me,
Stay a minute can't you see that:

Verse 3.

Too many hearts are broken,
A lover's promise never came with a maybe.
So many words are left unspoken,
The silent voices are driving me crazy.
As for all the pain you caused me,
Making up could never be your intention.
You'll never know how much you hurt me,
Stay can't you see that:

SWEET CHILD O' MINE

Words and Music by
W. AXL ROSE, SLASH, IZZY STRADLIN,
MICHAEL "DUFF" McKAGAN and STEVEN ADLER

Medium Rock ♩ = 122

*Recorded a half step lower.

1. She's got a smile____ that it seems to me____ re - minds____ me of child - hood
2. *See additional lyrics*

mem - o - ries, ____ where ev - 'ry - thing____ was as fresh____

as the bright blue sky.

Now and then when I see her face she takes me a-way to that

spe-cial place, and if I stared too long. I'll

prob-'ly break down and cry.

Additional Lyrics

2. She's got eyes of the bluest skies, as if they thought of rain.
   I hate to look into those eyes and see an ounce of pain.
   Her hair reminds me of a warm safe place where as a child I'd hide,
   And pray for the thunder and the rain to quietly pass me by. *(To Chorus)*

THESE ARE THE DAYS OF OUR LIVES

Words and Music by QUEEN

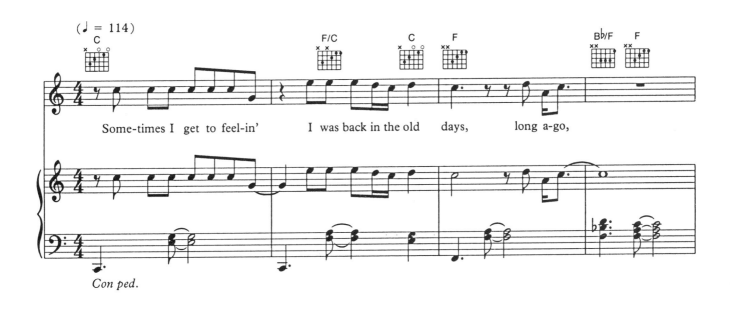

Some-times I get to feel-in' I was back in the old days, long a-go,

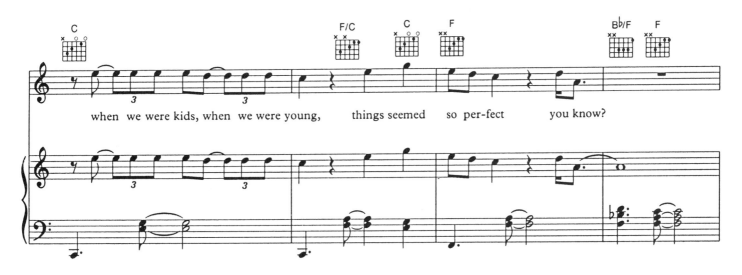

when we were kids, when we were young, things seemed so per-fect you know?

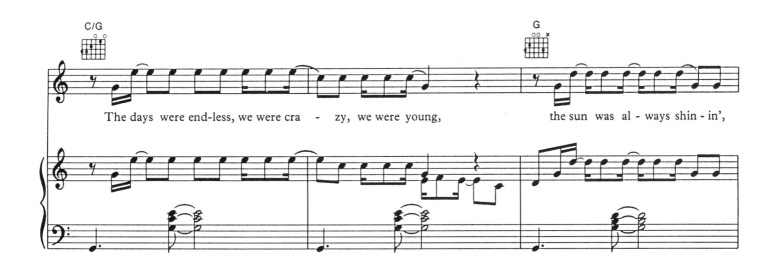

The days were end-less, we were cra - zy, we were young, the sun was al - ways shin - in',

Those were the days of our lives, yeah, the

days are___ all gone now_ but one thing's still true,_ when I

look and I find___ I still love you,

I still love you.

R.H.

Reproduced and printed by
Halstan & Co. Ltd., Amersham, Bucks., England